Little Creatures
Spiders

by Lisa J. Amstutz

raintree

a Capstone company — publishers for children

Raintree is an imprint of Capstone Global Library Limited, a company incorporated in England and Wales having its registered office at 264 Banbury Road, Oxford, OX2 7DY – Registered company number: 6695582

www.raintree.co.uk
myorders@raintree.co.uk

Edited by Gena Chester
Designed by Sarah Bennett
Picture research by Wanda Winch
Production by Tori Abraham
Originated by Capstone Global Library LTD
Printed and bound in India

ISBN 978 1 4747 4779 0 (hardback)
21 20 19 18 17
10 9 8 7 6 5 4 3 2 1

ISBN 978 1 4747 4783 7 (paperback)
22 21 20 19 18
10 9 8 7 6 5 4 3 2 1

British Library Cataloguing in Publication Data
A full catalogue record for this book is available from the British Library.

Acknowledgements
We would like to thank the following for permission to reproduce photographs:Dreamstime: G3miller, 17; Shutterstock: Aleksey Stemmer, spider web background, 3, 24, Calin Tatu, 9, Cathy Keifer, 11, 15, 19, Comel Constantin, 1, Dirk Ercken, 13, Jen Helton, cover, Panu Ruangjan, 5, Radka Palenikova, 22, RealNoi, 7, Worraket, 21

Every effort has been made to contact copyright holders of material reproduced in this book. Any omissions will be rectified in subsequent printings if notice is given to the publisher.

Contents

Many legs

Look!

It's a spider!

It has eight legs.

Its body has two parts.

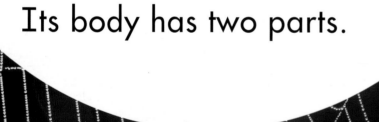

Some spiders are big.

Some are tiny.

Most have eight eyes.

Spiders make silk.

It is strong. It is sticky.

Silk makes spider webs.

Time to eat

Webs trap bugs.

Spiders eat the bugs.

Yum!

Some spiders hunt for food.

They hide and jump.

They eat frogs.

They eat mice too.

Munch!

Spiders bite their prey.

They have fangs.

fangs

Some spiders can bite people. Ouch!
But most will not hurt you.

Growing up

Spiders lay eggs.

A silk sac holds the eggs.

It keeps them safe.

Find out more

Insects and Spiders (Visual Explorers), Paul Calver and Toby Reynolds (Franklin Watts, 2016)

Spider (The Pet to Get), Rob Colson (Wayland, 2014)

Spiders (Really Weird Creatures), Clare Hibbert (Franklin Watts, 2015)

Websites

http://www.dkfindout.com/uk/animals-and-nature/arachnids/spiders/
Find information about photographs on this website.

www.zsl.org/zsl-london-zoo/exhibits/in-with-the-spiders/spider-facts
Visit London Zoo's website to read amazing facts about spiders.

Critical thinking questions

1. Why do spiders make webs?
2. What do spiders eat?
3. What is a fang?

Index